The Eating Illness Workbook

The Eating Illness

Workbook

By Joan Ebbitt, M.S.W.

Living Solutions
P.O. Box 616, Cork, Ireland.

Tel: INT'L Code + 353 21 4314300
Fax: INT'L Code + 353 21 4961269

e-mail: livhaz@indigo.ie
Website: www.livingsolutions.ie

HAZELDEN®

INFORMATION & EDUCATIONAL SERVICES

Hazelden
Center City, Minnesota 55012-0176

©1987 by Hazelden Foundation
All rights reserved. Published 1994 by
Hazelden Foundation. First published 1987
by Parkside Medical Services Corporation
Printed in the United States of America
No portion of this publication may be
reproduced in any manner without the
written permission of the publisher

ISBN: 1-56838-067-4

To all those who still suffer

Acknowledgments

I wish to thank the following people who helped to make this workbook possible. Gina Priestly, M.Ed., my teacher and friend, with all her heart encouraged me to do what I needed to do along the way. David B. Altman, M.D. taught me to live in the process, one day at a time. Kathy Dwyer, A.C.S.W., Peg O'Hare, C.S.A.C., and Lee Adams, A.C.S.W., were first to use the activities in this workbook with their patients. Kathy Leck, R.N., M.S., and John Small, M.A., advised and assisted with the final touches of this workbook.

Contents

Preface

Many men and women have developed patterns of eating that are at best inadequate and at worst dangerous to health and potentially life threatening. Statistics indicate that a growing number of individuals, perhaps as high as twenty-five percent of the population, are suffering from some form of compulsive eating behavior. Those who experience the cycles of binge-purge syndrome, compulsive overeating, starving, or a combination of these eating patterns, have an addiction to this behavior and to the foods they use in that they show signs of tolerance and withdrawal when practicing these behaviors. In addition, these compulsive eaters often have a distorted body image. They obsess about their weight and their body size.

This workbook discusses the compulsive eating behaviors and gives the reader/worker information and education regarding eating problems. The words "eating illness," "eating disorders," and "eating problems" are used interchangeably throughout the text. A variety of terms are used in order to emphasize a broad spectrum of troubled eating patterns.

JOAN EBBITT

Eating disorders exist when a person's use of food and rituals and practices surrounding the use of food cause increasingly serious problems in major areas of the person's life. If one's eating pattern is interfering in her life in any way, she probably has an eating disorder. The eating disorder manifests itself in various ways.

Most people who have eating disorders follow a pattern of both overeating and undereating. Some overeat and then purge themselves in various ways such as vomiting or using laxatives. Others overeat and gain excessive weight. Still others overeat and then starve themselves. Still other individuals only starve themselves.

These disordered eating behaviors are all forms of the same disease. This disease involves a pathological use of food that is sometimes coupled with addictive rituals or unhealthy practices surrounding food use. The disease could properly be called the "eating illness."

The readings, activities, and exercises in this workbook are designed to bring you face to face with your eating disorder and the pain and problems it causes in your life. If you take the time to read, reflect upon, and talk about the symptoms of your eating illness, you will find relief from the consequences of compulsive eating. You will experience hope for recovery.

Work Hard!

Jessica

When Jessica was five or six years old, she began to gain weight. One of her favorite pastimes was to eat dinner with her friends. She loved picnics with her family and had the most fun when she went out for ice cream with her brothers and sisters. Even as a young child she loved sandwiches, sweet rolls, and snacks with salty or sweet tastes.

Soon Jessica's mother restricted her calories and placed Jessica on a diet. Jessica hated it. Soon she began to sneak food...

Gina

At thirteen, Gina, who was about five pounds overweight, decided to go "on a diet." She quickly lost five pounds and loved her new look. Gazing into the mirror, she decided to lose another five pounds so she could "look even better."

By the time her parents began to notice, Gina had lost nineteen pounds. She was no longer eating meals with her family and she told her parents that she couldn't be home at mealtime "due to school activities." Gina loved her new look. She couldn't understand why her parents were worried that she was "becoming anorexic."

THE TRUTH?

Charlie

At 2:30 a.m., Bob heard noises coming from the bathroom. He thought he heard someone vomiting and wondered if his roommate, Charlie, was sick. He waited a few minutes while he heard flushing sounds several times, followed by the sound of running water. Then he got out of bed and made his way down the hall.

Bob tapped on the bathroom door and called, "Charlie, are you okay?" Charlie opened the door and came out looking perfectly all right. He apologized for waking Bob and said that he was fine. He told Bob that something was wrong with the toilet and said he would call the plumber in the morning.

At breakfast the next day, Bob couldn't find the two dozen donuts he had bought the day before. He wondered if Charlie had given the donuts away. Bob made a mental note to ask Charlie about the donuts...

Stephanie

Stephanie stood in the dressing room of the "Large and Lively Women's Store." Tears rolled down her face. Size 26-½ would no longer zip over her hips.

In disgust, Stephanie promised that this was it! No more being overweight! She would go on a diet, eat sensibly, and lose 100 pounds. Enough was enough! All she had to do was set her mind to the task.

She looked in the mirror and said aloud, "Stephanie, you are going to lose weight. You are going to be beautiful! You are going to be *thin*!" Feeling better, she got dressed, left the dressing room, and walked out of the store with her head held high.

It was later in the day than she realized. Dinner time was past. Stephanie drove to the nearest fast-food place to order the salad bar. When she arrived, however, the salad bar looked picked over. Stephanie hesitated and then said, "I'll have a couple of burgers, fries, and a malt. It's too late to start my diet today. I'll start my diet tomorrow."

The Strongest Woman in the World...

These scenarios reflect some symptoms of eating disorders. There are some clues and even blatant examples of compulsive overeating, binge eating, starving, or vomiting after binge eating. These are only a few of the symptoms of eating disorders.

Many different symptoms can indicate an eating illness. Two of the most prominent symptoms are *obsession about food use* and *obsession about one's body size*. Many more signs of the eating illness, however, can be identified as one begins to realize that his or her eating is causing some life problems.

The following readings and exercises will be helpful in discovering additional symptoms of the eating illness. These exercises present an opportunity for you to think about the problems that compulsive eating has caused in your life. You will be encouraged to share your findings with others who are recovering from eating disorders or other addictive illnesses.

Be Honest!

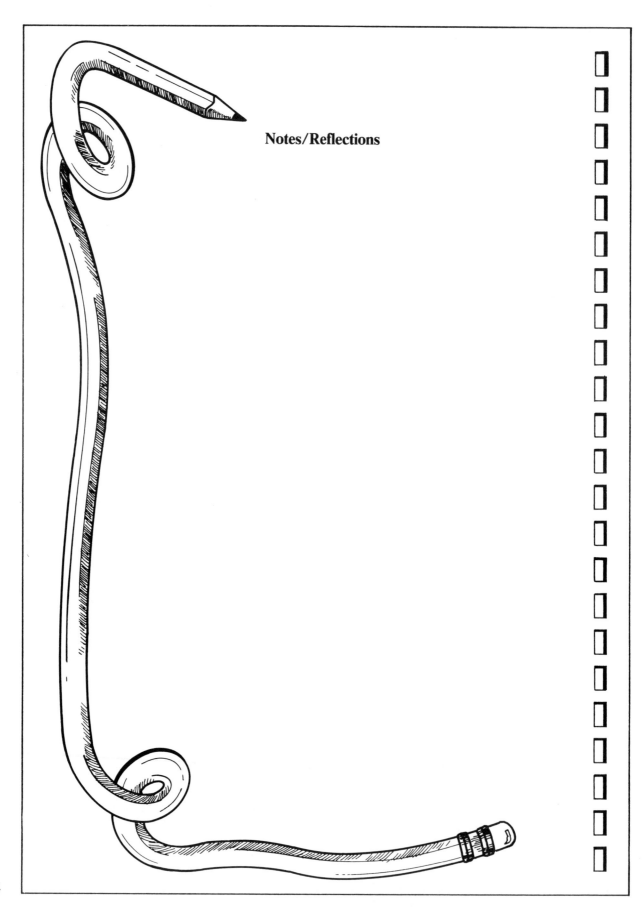

Notes/Reflections

COMPULSIVE EATING

2

Compulsive eating is eating in a way that you do not *intend* to eat. It is eating when you don't plan to eat. It is eating at the wrong time and/or in the wrong place.

This illness progresses slowly. Often compulsive eaters are not even aware that the sickness is present. It is characterized by a chronic, underlying urge to eat that, once experienced, remains for an indefinite period of time. The compulsive eater may experience short periods when her eating behavior is under control, but once compulsive overeating patterns have been established, the urge to eat will return again and again.

After this urge to eat has become firmly entrenched in the compulsive overeater, loss of control over one's eating behavior can be identified. Loss of control over eating behavior means that one can no longer eat *according to intention or nutritional need.*

Consider the following eating pattern of the typical compulsive overeater:

She begins her day with a promise that today she will start her diet. She will probably eat a meager breakfast or no breakfast at all, thus setting the compulsive eating syndrome in motion. By 10:00 a.m., however, she will be experiencing genuine hunger. With the onset of the "urge to eat," she may give herself permission to have "just one" sweet roll. But, as soon as she has consumed the sweet roll, she gives herself this message: "I blew it! I may as well eat whatever I want today and diet tomorrow." Her lunch then consists of a double hamburger, large fries, a milkshake, and a piece of pie. The afternoon break finds her at the candy machine, and after work she stops at the grocery store to get a "few things I need," including sweet and salty snacks or whatever pleases her whim. That evening at home she eats everything she bought at the store.

The following morning, she awakens and promises herself, "Today I will diet..." But, when 10:00 o'clock rolls around, she once again has "just one" sweet roll. No matter what she says or does, she cannot break the cycle of eating too much and then not enough. She doesn't realize that she has an illness called compulsive eating, in which she lives in a perpetual pattern of eating too much, not enough, too much, not enough, too much, and not enough in a chronic pattern of compulsive eating.

Use the following space to describe *your* compulsive eating behavior. Tell about a typical day in which your compulsive eating was active:

_____

_____

_____

_____

_____

_____

_____

_____

_____

_____

_____

_____

_____

_____

_____

_____

_____

_____

_____

_____

_____

_____

_____

_____

_____

_____

FOOD PATTERN

A. Describe the average daily amounts of food you eat; name the foods you eat and your pattern of eating (Example: 3 meals, all day or night eating, etc.).

_____

_____

_____

B. Do you binge? _____ How often? _____

On what foods? _____

_____

C. Do you starve? _____ What is your pattern? Explain. _____

_____

D. Do you do any of the following? Explain.

1. Vomit? _____

_____

2. Use laxatives? _____

_____

3. Feel guilty after eating? _____

_____

4. Fast? _____

_____

5. Become irritable before meals? _____

_____

6. Promise yourself or others that you will diet? _____

_____

7. Eat until your stomach feels pain, but continue to eat anyway? ____

   _____

8. Hide food? _____

9. Have family problems due to your eating/or not eating? _____

   _____

10. Take diet pills? _____

    _____

11. Take diet shots? _____

12. Go to weight loss clinics? _____ How many? _____

    _____

13. Think about your weight all the time? _____

    _____

14. Feel embarrassed about your body size? _____

    _____

15. Binge on foods made with refined sugar? _____

    _____

16. Binge on foods made with with flour? _____

    _____

17. Avoid discussing your eating problems with others? _____

    _____

18. Have physical problems due to eating disorder (example: esophageal, stomach, or bowel problems, etc.)? Explain. _____

    _____

19. Abuse alcohol? _____

Please use the following to write your eating history. Tell about your loss of control in regard to food use or rituals and practices surrounding your food use. Share your eating history with another person.

Consider the following:

1. Kinds, amounts, and frequency of food use.

2. Foggy memories or difficulty concentrating after eating too much.

3. Feeling high after vomiting or starving.

4. Behavior changes
    a. Mood swings with eating/not eating.
    b. Withdrawal from others to eat or starve.

5. Rituals surrounding food use
    a. Overeating or binge eating on certain foods.
    b. Frequent eating out.
    c. Sneak eating.
    d. Weighing self daily or more often.

6. Preoccupation
    a. Thinking about eating/not eating.
    b. Eating for relief from problems, boredom, frustration, etc.
    c. Protecting your food supply; hiding food.
    d. Preoccupation with body size.

7. Attempts to control eating and/or weight
    a. Doctor's diets.
    b. Fad diets.
    c. Diet pills and/or shots.
    d. Starving, vomiting, laxative use, and/or manual extraction of stool.
    e. Diet clubs or fat farms.
    f. Hypnosis, acupuncture, stomach stapling, and/or gastric bypass surgery.
    g. Spending money to control eating or weight.

8. Family and/or social difficulties
   a. Others trying to control your eating behavior.
   b. Loss of interest in outside activities.
   c. Lack of social life.
   d. Sexual problems.

9. Spiritual difficulties
   a. Relationships with others and/or God avoided due to excessive preoccupation with food and/or your body.
   b. Loss of self-esteem.
   c. Guilt over eating behavior.

10. Job problems
    a. Loss of job due to eating behavior.
    b. Inability to concentrate at work.
    c. Absenteeism and/or tardiness due to eating patterns.
    d. Time off work due to problems related to eating, starving, and/or vomiting such as visits to the dentist for tooth or gum problems, problems with heart, bowels, or colon, etc.

11. Serious life problems
    a. Depression.
    b. Suicide attempts.
    c. Accidents related to eating/not eating.

Use the following space to write your eating history:

_____

_____

_____

_____

_____

_____

_____

_____

_____

_____

_____

_____

_____

_____

_____

_____

_____

_____

_____

_____

_____

_____

_____

_____

_____

etc...

13

EATING DISORDER SYMPTOMS

5

Place a mark next to each symptom that you have ever experienced. ✓

____ Eating for relief.

____ Starving occasionally.

____ Always feeling too full after meals.

____ Feeling guilty about amounts of food eaten.

____ Clothes become too small.

____ More frequent eating for relief.

____ Binge eating on certain "trigger foods."

____ Increasing tolerance for quantities of food.

____ Feeling groggy after eating.

____ Sneaking food.

____ Hiding food.

____ Visiting diet doctor.

____ Taking diet pills.

____ Starving increases.

____ Vomiting begins.

____ Others tell you to lose weight.

____ Avoiding discussing food problems.

____ Losing weight.

____ Rationalizing and making alibis.

____ Vomiting daily or more often.

____ Guilt feelings related to eating behavior.

____ Regaining weight and/or adding to former weight.

____ Increased amounts of time spent in bathroom to move bowels.

____ Manual extraction of feces.

____ Feeling ashamed of body size.

____ Changing eating patterns.

____ Exercising to excess.

____ Seeking help from psychiatry, counseling, or group therapy.

____ Work problems.

____ Constant depression.

____ Persistent remorse.

____ Beginning a new diet every morning.

____ Physical problems (stomach, bowel, heart, back, and/or leg problems, etc.).

____ Constant binge/starve pattern.

_____ Weighing yourself daily or more often.

_____ Going on fad diets.

_____ Laxative abuse.

_____ Loss of control over food use.

_____ Unable to stop starving.

_____ Breaking promises and resolutions.

_____ Loss of control over vomiting or use of laxatives.

_____ Eating in the middle of the night.

_____ Moral deterioration (stealing food, etc.).

_____ Impaired thinking.

_____ Round-the-clock eating.

_____ Feeling totally isolated.

_____ Obsession with thoughts of food and shame about body size.

_____ Admits complete defeat.

Use the following space to write a statement about each of the Eating Disorder Symptoms that you checked on the previous page:

_____

_____

_____

_____

_____

_____

_____

_____

_____

_____

_____

_____

_____

_____

_____

_____

_____

_____

_____

_____

_____

_____

_____

_____

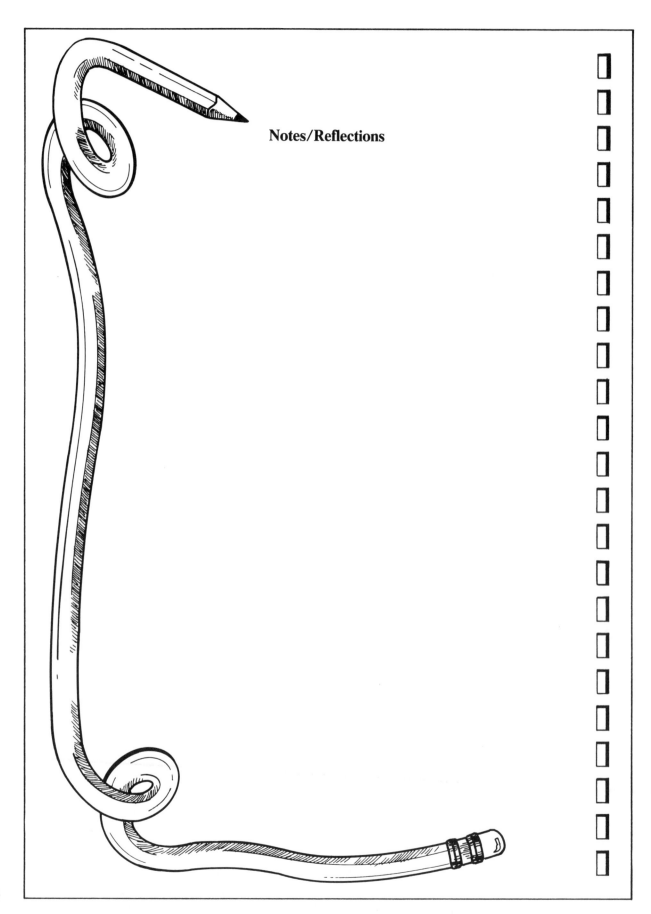

Notes/Reflections

HARMFUL CONSEQUENCES

Eating disorders exist when a person's use of food or rituals and practices surrounding the use of food cause increasingly serious problems in the major areas of one's life.

Please list the harmful consequences of your eating illness in the spaces below. Explain how your eating behavior hurts you or causes you pain in the following life areas.

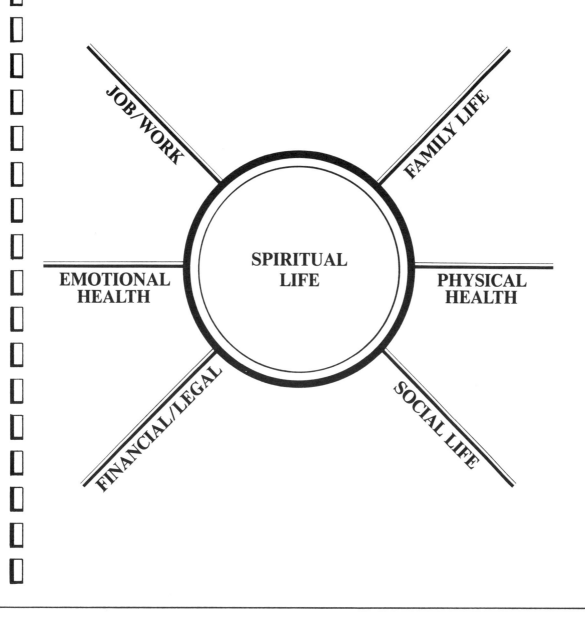

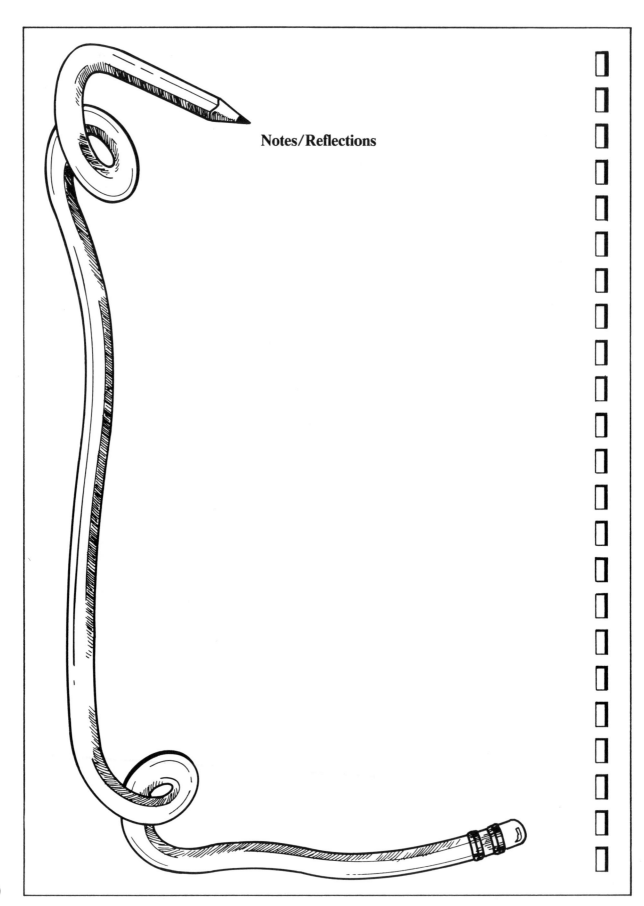

Notes/Reflections

*The real problem is not your weight... it is your eating!

Many people who have eating disorders have often told themselves, "I just want to lose a little weight." Another idea they begin to believe is, "When I get thin, I will be happy." These and many other fantasies contribute to the advancing progress of the eating illness.

In reality, people who suffer with eating disorders generally follow two eating patterns. In the first pattern, not enough food is eaten. In the second pattern, too much food is eaten. Most compulsive eaters swing back and forth between these two patterns, first eating too much and then not eating enough food.

Learning to be abstinent means that the compulsive eater must begin eating in an entirely new way. It means that she will begin to accept the fact that the compulsive swing pattern will be broken when *the right amount* and *the right kind* of foods are eaten. It means that the body will return to (or stay at) the proper weight.

Some people who practice this way of eating say that it involves learning to eat without feeling guilty once the eating is done. Others say that eating with abstinence has brought new physical and emotional benefits, including more energy and improved clarity of thought. Most people recovering from an eating illness begin to feel a new sense of stability.

Generally, people who begin to eat in an abstinent manner stop eating foods made with refined sugars and carbohydrates. Many stop eating white and enriched flour. Many reduce the fat content in their foods.

The most important element in learning to be abstinent is developing a *plan*. If meals are carefully planned, then the chances for that quick, compulsive snack will be lessened. Some individuals include one or several planned snacks in addition to regularly planned daily meals as a way to reduce the urge to eat compulsively. The key is to plan!

When the compulsive eater begins to abstain from overeating or undereating, she usually experiences feelings of inner peace and serenity. If she is working on a spiritual recovery through the Twelve Steps of Overeaters Anonymous at the same time, her chances for staying abstinent and serene are enhanced. She begins to experience the miracle of real sobriety!

Use the following space to describe how you feel about abstinence.

_____

_____

_____

_____

_____

_____

_____

_____

_____

In what areas of abstinence do you need more help?

_____

_____

_____

_____

_____

_____

_____

_____

_____

Most people who have eating disorders initially believe that "everything will be fine when I change my weight." Similarly, most alcoholics initially believe that "everything will be fine if I don't get drunk." Both the alcoholic and the compulsive eater who believe these statements are suffering from *denial* of the real problems.

In the case of alcoholism, the addicted individual must finally come to believe that the drinking itself is the problem. Taking the first drink is the action that eventually leads to the consequences of getting drunk. In order to get better, the alcoholic must begin to believe that the problem lies in the *actual act of the drinking itself*. Getting drunk is only the *result* of the drinking.

It is the same with eating disorders. A compulsive eater operates under the illusion that changing one's weight will solve the problem. She tells herself, "When I get thin, I'll be okay." Even when there is no medical or other physical reason to lose weight, she still believes she must "get thin" to be happy.

What the compulsive eater fails to recognize is that it is the *actual act of eating* (or, in some cases, not eating) that leads to the consequence of being unhappy about one's weight. In order to get better, the compulsive eater must recognize that his or her *eating behavior* is the real problem that needs to be changed.

If the alcoholic accepts that there is a drinking problem, then the action to stop drinking will stop the consequences of getting drunk. If the compulsive eater accepts that there is an eating problem, then the action to stop eating compulsively will stop the consequences of maintaining the improper weight. Letting go of denial means that the alcoholic will be able to admit and accept the fact that he or she has a *drinking* problem. The compulsive eater will be able to admit and accept the fact that he or she has an *eating* problem.

What does this mean to you? Explain in the following space:

_____

_____

_____

_____

_____

_____

_____

_____

_____

_____

_____

_____

_____

_____

_____

_____

_____

_____

_____

_____

_____

_____

Most people can identify a person who is in the late stages of anorexia. It is easy to see a person whose body is so painfully thin that it is emaciated and to recognize that the individual is in a state of starvation. In the late stages, the anorexic often begins to lose her hair. She often acts as if she is in a trance. Her behavior becomes dream-like and ethereal. These unusual behaviors are a result of starving herself.

In reality, anorexia begins long before the telltale signs can be recognized. The main symptom of the disease is a *fear of becoming fat*. As the illness grows, so does the fear of fatness.

If you are suffering from the disease of anorexia you may find that you are preoccupied with your body size. You will also notice that you think about food constantly. In the early stages of your illness, you may practice binge eating and then fast from food for short periods of time. You may fool yourself and your family and friends because no one (including yourself) could believe that anyone who eats such large quantities of food could be anorexic.

What you have not realized, however, is that the symptoms of anorexia include the same signs of all eating illnesses: obsession with food and preoccupation with body size. You try harder and harder to "control" your eating. Finally, when you are able to go for days without eating any food, you feel proud of yourself. What an accomplishment! To actually be able to control your desire to eat until you stop eating altogether is your greatest achievement. At least that is what you believe if you have anorexia.

Unfortunately, however, as your illness progresses you become less and less able to stop starving yourself. Eventually, your mind and body become dangerously weak. Even when family and friends become worried and beg you to resume eating, you cannot change your pattern of not eating and overcontrolling your starving. And therein lies the baffling nature of anorexia.

As an anorexic, you have no idea that you are powerless over your compulsive eating behavior. But reflect on what happens to you when family, friends, and even medical personnel tell you that you must resume eating or die from starvation. Suddenly you find that you cannot just stop starving and return to normal eating. Again and again you promise that you will eat, only to discover that the act of eating has become so repulsive to you that it is nearly impossible. For the first time, you may begin to realize that your starving is *out of control* rather than *under your control.*

There is, however, another complicating factor: your distorted view of your body size. Again and again your friends and loved ones tell you that you have become "too thin." But your response is that they are wrong. Sometimes you tell yourself that your friends and loved ones are "jealous" because they don't have bodies that are thin and beautiful like your own. This *inability to see your body as others see it* contributes to your progressing anorexia.

Recovery from this illness means that you must accept the fact that you have a great deal in common with obese people and with people of normal weight who binge and purge. It may be shocking for you to read this. Your insides may scream, "No! No! I am not like those others!" In reality, however, all persons with eating disorders are obsessed with food and obsessed with their body size. In order to recover from your eating disorder, you must accept the fact that you are obsessed and that you need help from others who are recovering from the same illness.

Review the symptoms of anorexia as listed below and then describe your symptoms and how they progressed.

Signs of anorexia: Check the ones that apply to you:

_____ 1. Extreme fear of fatness.

_____ 2. Preoccupation with body size.

_____ 3. Alternate periods of starving and then eating, with the starving time gradually increasing.

_____ 4. Preoccupation with cooking or preparing food, often fixing elaborate meals for others without actually eating.

_____ 5. Loss of 25 percent of one's body fat (late stage).

_____ 6. Occasional (sometimes frequent) purging of food by vomiting, laxative abuse, or diuretics. (As the starving increases, many anorexics no longer purge themselves.)

_____ 7. Others are concerned that you are becoming too thin.

_____ 8. Promises to loved ones to resume eating with inability to achieve the new eating behavior.

Discuss your symptoms here in the following space:

_____

_____

_____

_____

_____

_____

etc...

The popular conception of bulimia is that it is an illness in which people eat a great deal of food and then vomit. It is a surprise then to learn that many people who have bulimia do not vomit or purge themselves in any other way. Some individuals with bulimia simply eat a great deal of food and then become obese.

The main feature of bulimia is *binge eating*. Bulimics suffer from the urge to eat great amounts of food and usually eat the food quickly. Often they hide the eating behavior from others. Sometimes, when the binge is over the bulimic will become tired and fall asleep. At other times, the bulimic will stop eating because ingesting food begins to become physically painful. Many bulimics purge themselves by vomiting or using diuretics or laxatives.

If you have bulimia, you probably feel guilty about your binge eating. You have promised yourself again and again that you will stop eating so much food. Filled with shame and embarrassment, you have probably tried to diet or even fast from food altogether. Unable to be successful, you may have gone underground with your binge eating so that no one else will see how you are hurting yourself.

You probably know very well that your eating pattern is not normal. No doubt you are afraid that you can never stop this eating pattern. When you feel discouraged, you eat even more food to escape the pain and then feel even worse.

If you have some of the symptoms of bulimia, please describe them in the space below. Describe your eating binges and tell how you feel after a binge.

_____

_____

_____

_____

_____

_____

_____

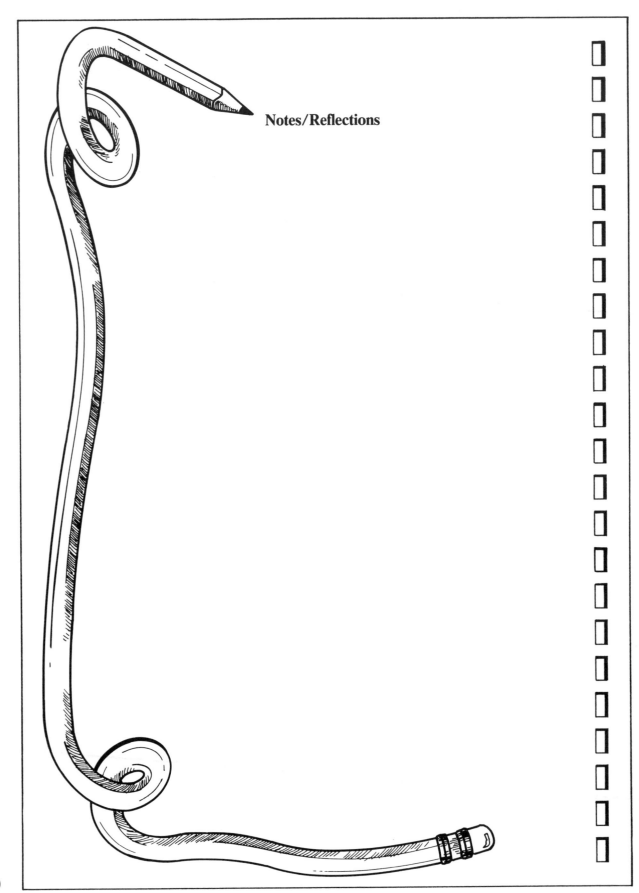

Notes/Reflections

PHYSICAL CRAVING: WHAT'S WRONG WITH MY BODY? 11

What do you always want to eat? What foods trigger you to keep eating more once you begin to eat them? What foods do you miss most when you are "dieting"?

As you ponder these questions, you may begin to realize that the foods you crave have a high content of sugar, flour, or fat. These types of foods seem to be the greatest source of difficulty for compulsive eaters.

When you eat these foods you often find that after you eat the first bite, it becomes difficult to stop eating. Even when you have promised that you will have "just one," after tasting a trigger food you tell yourself, "I'll have just a little bit more." If you stop eating the food, your body craves that food even more.

Use the following spaces to describe the foods that trigger physical craving for you:

SUGAR FOODS	FLOUR FOODS	HIGH-FAT FOODS

Tell what it is like to try to eat "just a little" of the foods you crave.

_____

_____

_____

_____

_____

_____

_____

_____

_____

_____

_____

_____

_____

_____

_____

_____

_____

_____

_____

_____

_____

_____

Use this page to have a "conversation" with your body. Start by placing your name in the first blank space. Address your body directly as if you were talking to another person. Then let your body "talk back to you." Consider the following example:

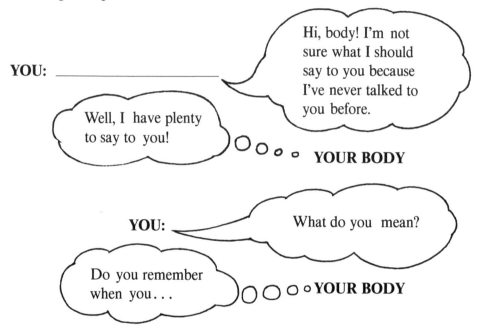

YOU: _____

Hi, body! I'm not sure what I should say to you because I've never talked to you before.

Well, I have plenty to say to you!

YOUR BODY

YOU:

What do you mean?

Do you remember when you...

YOUR BODY

As you can see, this assignment will help you to "hear" what your body needs to tell you about your eating behavior or about other issues regarding your eating illness. Record a brief conversation with your body in the following space, and then don't reread the conversation until you share it with your group or another person.

_____
_____
_____
_____
_____
_____
_____

Keep talking . . .

_____

_____

_____

_____

_____

_____

_____

_____

_____

_____

_____

_____

_____

_____

_____

_____

_____

_____

_____

_____

_____

_____

_____

_____

Following the directions on page 33 for "A Conversation with Your Body," have a "conversation" with one or all of the following: Trust, Faith, Higher Power or God, and Fear.

_____

_____

_____

_____

_____

_____

_____

_____

_____

_____

_____

_____

_____

_____

_____

_____

_____

_____

_____

_____

_____

_____

_____

_____

A CONVERSATION WITH _____

_____
_____
_____
_____
_____
_____
_____
_____
_____
_____
_____
_____
_____
_____
_____
_____
_____
_____
_____
_____
_____
_____
_____
_____
_____

BODY IMAGE

Have you ever told yourself, "I feel so fat!," only to hear a friend respond, "You're not fat!" You were probably glad to hear your friend tell you that you are not fat, even if you didn't believe her. And even if you heard ten people tell you that you were not fat, it would still be hard to believe.

You don't believe the way any other person describes your body because one of the symptoms of your eating disorder is that you distort the way you see yourself. If you are fat, you may look into the mirror and see yourself as thinner than you really are, or you may see yourself as fatter than you are. Normal-weight or underweight individuals who have eating disorders generally see themselves as being seriously overweight.

This is a common symptom of eating illness. And it is a dangerous symptom because it distorts reality and makes you unable to see how you *really* look. People with eating disorders perceive their bodies in a way that constitutes denial of their illness. You have not been able to see the actual weight and size of your body, and when others describe your body, you often feel surprised.

As you begin to recover from your eating illness, you will need to rely on others to help you to let go of distorted perceptions of your body. Trust is an essential tool. Trust that others will tell you the truth about how you look. Trust your peers in treatment groups and at Overeaters Anonymous. They can help you to begin to see your body as it really is.

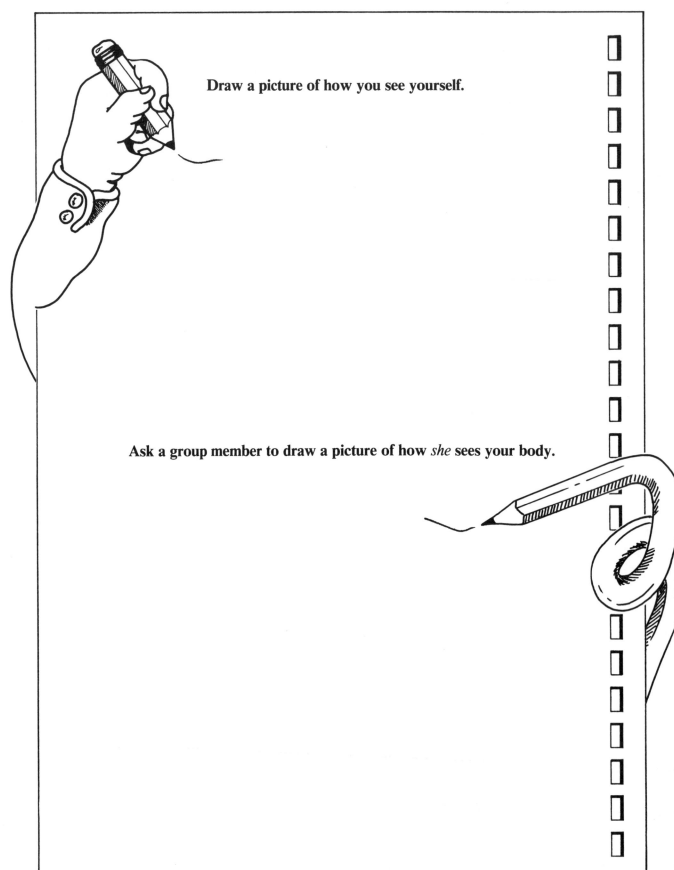

Draw a picture of how you see yourself.

Ask a group member to draw a picture of how *she* sees your body.

Recovering from your eating illness means that you will begin to accept yourself as you are now. It means that you will nurture yourself by following your food plan. You will stop trying to cover up your body by wearing clothes that "hide" your size. You will learn to be comfortable with your body.

Here is a prayer or meditation that you can say each day to help you to accept your body. Memorize it. Say this prayer while bathing each day.

Prayer

Body, you are a gift from God. I love you because you are the vessel that holds my spirit. You are lovely, inside and outside.

God, help me to treat my body with love and respect. Grant me the courage to care for the wounds of my eating problems with the grace of abstinence. I give thanks for this miracle of new energy that gives my body, mind, and spirit new life. Amen.

Perhaps you want to write your own prayer or meditation. Memorize it and pray it daily.

_____

_____

_____

_____

_____

_____

_____

_____

_____

_____

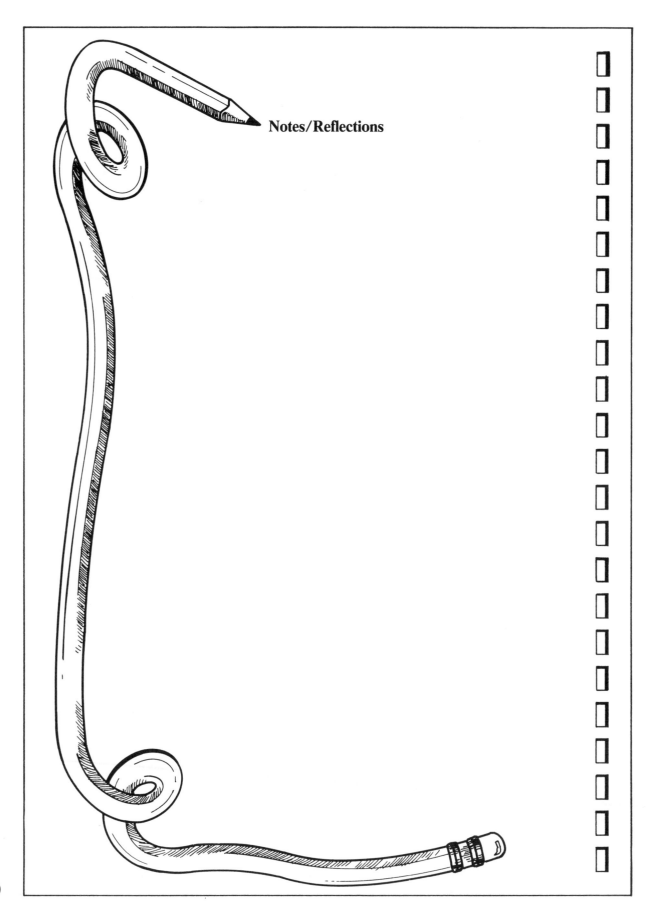

Notes/Reflections

You may have been suffering from your eating disorder long enough to have developed serious problems with your ability to digest food or eliminate wastes from your body. Perhaps you have no idea that your eating illness could be responsible for your stomach or bowel disorders. Maybe you have tried to ignore your physical problems or to keep them secret from others because you feel embarrassed to ask for help.

The compulsive eating pattern of eating too much food and then not eating enough frequently causes physical problems. Many who come into treatment complain of constipation or diarrhea or alternating periods of both problems. Some experience symptoms of colitis, and others have hemorrhoids. Still others find that they have generalized periods of nausea or inability to hold food down if they have been vomiting.

Some people with eating disorders completely lose their ability to control the rectal muscle that controls elimination. At times, some individuals begin to experience constant diarrhea, and with each period of eating they may be unable to retain the food but will have an instant bowel movement. Others begin to have the opposite problem of becoming unable to eliminate waste at all.

In this latter case, some people begin to remove their bodily waste by hand. They remove feces manually by inserting a finger into the rectum to assist in the extraction of the stool. Eventually, this means of moving the bowels becomes the only way that some people with eating disorders can pass waste. These individuals become addicted to moving their bowels in this manner.

As the need to extract the stool manually increases, one may experience a feeling of sexual excitement as the extraction takes place. This sexual stimulation, coupled with the distaste of admitting that one is handling one's feces, makes this eating disorder symptom extremely difficult to admit. Feelings of guilt, shame, and embarrassment often stop the suffering person from telling others or from asking for help to stop this behavior. She may not realize that this behavior is a result of her eating disorder, and so she keeps her secret and wonders why she continues to behave in a way that she thinks is "shameful."

If you are suffering from this symptom, it is important that you share your secret and ask for help to stop the behavior. As you learn to eat a healthy food plan, your bowels can return to their normal function.

When you tell this secret to your group, you will probably feel relieved that your secret is out. You will have the chance to get better because you are no longer harboring a secret.

If you have problems with digestion or elimination, please write them here. Then discuss the problems in your group therapy.

_____

_____

_____

_____

_____

_____

_____

_____

_____

_____

_____

_____

_____

_____

_____

_____

_____

_____

THE PROBLEM OF OBSESSION:
WHAT'S WRONG WITH MY HEAD?

17

One of the symptoms of eating disorders is that the sick person begins to think about one or all of the following: food, losing weight, and body size. Eventually, the preoccupation becomes a constant companion. Half or more of the person's waking hours are spent thinking about eating or not eating, gaining or losing weight, or observing one's body to check one's size. After a while, the thoughts become so constant that thinking about normal, routine activities becomes almost impossible. The mental obsession begins to interfere with one's work, home life, social activities, and spirituality.

In the following space, write a paragraph describing your mental obsession with food and/or body size:

_____

_____

_____

_____

_____

_____

_____

_____

_____

_____

_____

_____

_____

_____

_____

_____

_____

_____

_____

_____

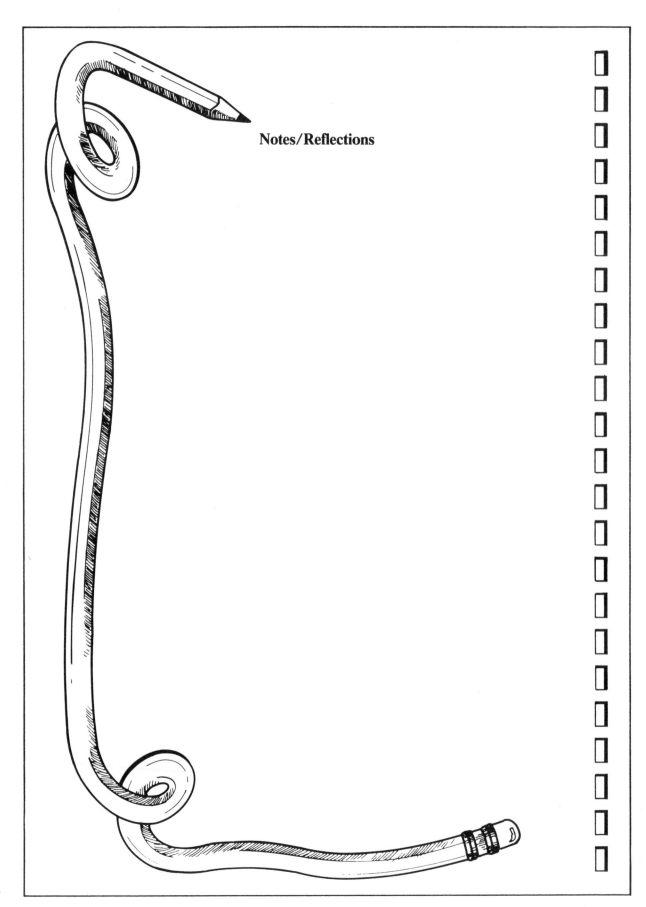

Notes/Reflections

"That weight balance program didn't work. What I need is a good diet. Maybe I'll skip breakfast and lunch today, fast all day Sunday, and lose forty pounds. . . .I probably wouldn't eat like this if my job were easier. . . .That's it! I'll quit my job and move to California. There's plenty of fresh fruit there, good, green, leafy vegetables. . . .I'll be fine! Wait a minute, though. I can't afford to buy a house in California. . . .I know, I'll move out of my apartment and buy a cute little house in the neighborhood. I'll put a microwave oven in the kitchen so I can cook fast when I get home from work. Yeah, that's it! I'll just zap up a little chicken and vegetables in the microwave. . . .But my friends hate microwave cooking, so if I do that they won't come over anymore. Oh, well, they don't come over anyway. . . .They don't want to be around me. . .Mary said I have an eating problem. . . .She's crazy. She's just jealous because I went out with her old boyfriend. . . .I know, that's what I'll do! I'll call Tom, and everything will be all right. . . ."

If you recognize this thinking pattern as your own, you have just discovered another symptom of your eating disorder: a "spinning" thought pattern. That fast, rapid movement from thought to thought is a common sign that you have an eating illness. And that kind of thinking keeps you from living in reality and perpetuates your eating illness.

The result of your spinning thoughts is that you are always brooding about your past or dreaming about your future. Usually, you think back to your past eating problems and blame others for your lack of success in changing your eating behavior. People with eating disorders often believe that "tough breaks" or "bad luck" kept them from being able to "control" their eating. They often feel sad or depressed.

Perhaps you, too, have developed a spinning thought pattern. Then you start dreaming about how you will change. You tell yourself that you will be different "tomorrow." Or you say, "I'll start my diet on Monday." Always you promise to change your eating "come New Year's Day." And you feel new strength as that new determination to change flows through you.

Even as that firm resolution to change is rushing through you, however, a terrible tragedy is happening in your life. You are missing *the reality of the present moment.* Even as you are dreaming about how you will be different "someday," you may be stuffing your mouth full of cookies. Or you may be on your way to the bathroom to vomit "just one more time." Because you are so busy thinking about the past or dreaming about the future, you miss every opportunity to stop the symptoms of your sickness *right now*.

You probably don't even notice that you are compulsively eating again. Or you don't see that you are growing dangerously thin because it "feels so good" to fast that you tell yourself that you will stop after you lose "just one more pound." That kind of thinking keeps you stuck in the grips of a serious illness because you are unable to see the truth about what is happening to you.

Spinning thinking prevents you from recognizing and preventing the consequences of your eating illness. It prevents you from realizing that you cannot stop eating or starving, vomiting, or taking amphetamines to diet. It sidetracks you with the "dream" that one day you will be different. And living in that insidious dream world prevents you from facing the truth that you are sick and need help to recover from your eating illness.

Spinning thinking can best be pictured in the following diagram:

PAST	SPINNING	FUTURE
2. "I had to eat because my childhood was awful."		1. "When I get thin I'll be okay."
4. "I couldn't get a boyfriend, so I ate."		3. "When I get a boyfriend, my life will be perfect."
5. "I binged and purged because I lost my job."		6. "When I lose 10 pounds, I'll be happy."

In a spinning thought pattern, the present moment is missed because your thoughts are always focused on the past or the future, never the present. Each number in the thought pattern diagram represents a rapid move from the idea of feeling sad that your past was full of hardships that "made you" binge eat or starve to the next idea of dreaming about how you will change in the future into a "beautiful, thin, and healthy person."

Soon your spinning thought pattern begins to carry over into all areas of your life. Often you may begin thinking so rapidly and erratically that every area of your life becomes seriously affected. You may begin to change jobs frequently or have difficulty in your relationships because you are so restless. A need for constant change may be the only steady pattern in your life.

When you become abstinent from compulsive eating or starving, you will slowly begin to realize that something in your thinking is changing. Many people begin to experience a new clarity of thought after following an abstinent food plan for only four or five days. You will notice that you will be less anxious, and you may feel less nervous or irritable. Your thought pattern often slows down, and you will pay better attention to what is happening in your life *right now*.

Many of you will find yourselves feeling more peaceful with your thoughts. As your period of abstinence from compulsive eating increases, you will come to realize that compulsive overthinking is one of the symptoms of your active eating disorder. And your newfound serenity will increase your desire to *remain* abstinent from compulsive eating.

Use the following space to describe your spinning thinking pattern. Describe how it prevented you from living in the present moment and taking control of your life and behavior.

_____

_____

_____

_____

_____

_____

SPIRITUAL DIFFICULTIES: WHAT'S WRONG WITH MY SPIRIT? 19

Compulsive overeating or undereating affects the way you feel and your relationships with yourself and other people. When you have just begun one of your diets, you may feel filled with hope and determination. In your pathological pursuit of thinness, you promise that you will "eat right this time."

Inevitably, however, you break your promise and resume your compulsive eating pattern again. Feelings of defeat and self-loathing haunt you. Your spirit sags with the burden of "failing" again. You avoid your family and friends because you can't carry out your plan and feel embarrassed or ashamed.

If that pattern becomes established in the individual with an eating disorder, the person's spiritual life will suffer. If being alive spiritually means that one is open and actively relating to other people and to God, then the sickness of the eating behavior that causes the individual to withdraw in shame will destroy the person's spirit.

Ask yourself, "What's wrong with my spirit?" How does my eating or not eating harm my spiritual relationships with people and with God? How is my spirit burdened by my eating disorder? Use the following space to describe the spiritual problems caused by your eating disorder:

_____

_____

_____

_____

_____

_____

_____

_____

_____

_____

_____

_____

_____

etc...

Create your own title for the poem below. What fits best for you?

THE URGE TO _____

Eat? Starve? Vomit? Diet? Fast? Take laxatives? Lie? Steal? Obsess?

It stalks me like the night terrors.
I can hear it calling me when I am
in the living room, bathroom,
dining room, or kitchen and even
in the backyard.
I don't hear it coming, but
suddenly it's there.
It surrounds me with a silence that
is deafening.
I sit quietly and it shouts.
I yell and scream and make noise,
and it talks to me under its breath.
It won't leave me alone; it is
always lurking.
All the while I try to push it
away, it pushes back harder.
But when I stop and turn toward
it and say,"I know you're here,"
it walks along beside me and leaves
me alone.

What is it like for you to live with the urge to eat (or to starve, vomit, or obsess)? Describe your feelings here:

_____

_____

_____

_____

_____

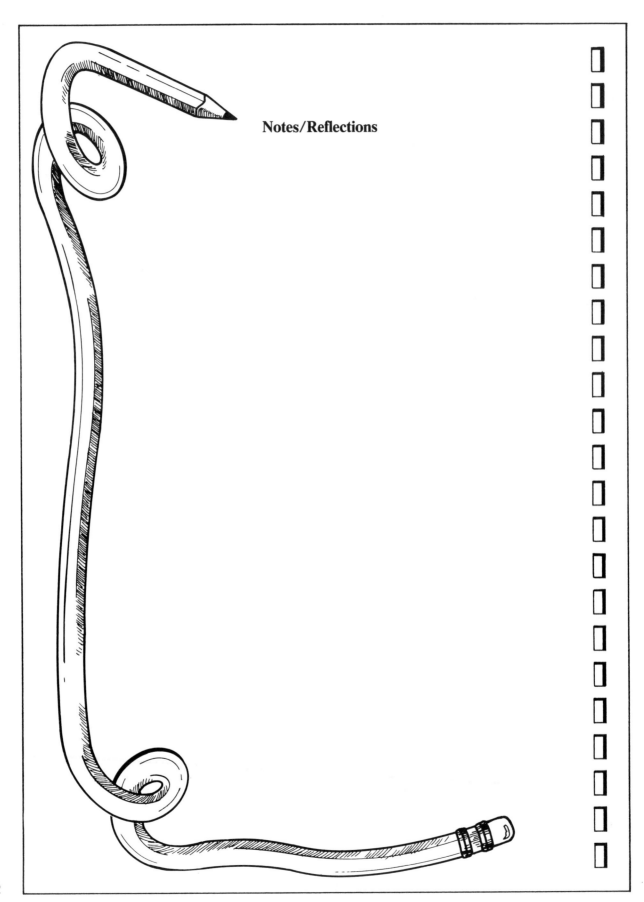

Notes/Reflections

Alice wondered if anyone else was afraid to talk about sex. She certainly didn't want to tell the group about her sexual worries and fears. It would be awful if her peers found out that she was unsure about her sexual orientation! She was thirty-three years old, and she told herself that she should know by now whether she was gay or straight!

Patti shifted uncomfortably in her seat feeling extremely embarrassed. She had been sexually involved with every man she had met for the past seven years. She used to wonder if it was normal to have sex with so many men. Sometimes she even felt addicted to sex and promiscuity.

Joe weighed 354 pounds. It was hard for him to fit in the chair. He didn't even want to be in the room. And he certainly didn't want to tell the group that he hadn't had any sexual experience in two years! His wife said she was "repulsed" by his body.

Sense of Self

"Wow! I can't believe what I am hearing!" Cindy listened to one of her fellow group members tell about being sexually abused by her father. She pondered her own history of incest. Her brother began to abuse her when she was nine years old. She felt guilty afterward and was afraid to tell her mother because Jack said he would hurt her if she told. Cindy wondered if she could begin to talk about it in her group.

At first Amy thought that she might be pregnant when she stopped having menstrual periods. After a few months, however, she knew she wasn't pregnant and began to wonder what was wrong. Then one day she overheard a friend tell someone else that a lot of running and dieting can cause menstruation to stop. Amy was glad to hear that because it made her know she was "really losing weight." She also heard her friend say something about anorexia, but Amy "knew" that that didn't apply to her! In any case, Amy certainly wasn't going to tell her group that her periods had stopped last year.

Don't be surprised if you relate to Alice's confusion, Patti's embarrassment, or Joe's shame. Maybe you have felt Cindy's fear. Dealing with issues about sexuality is not easy. Having an eating disorder complicates the problem.

Perhaps you have suffered from your eating disorder since childhood. You learned at an early age that eating (and sometimes not eating) could make you feel more comfortable or take away your fears or loneliness. When you begin to experience intense feelings, you may have learned to reach for food to calm yourself. If you did practice compulsive eating in your childhood, adolescence, or even adulthood, your eating illness may have prevented you from experiencing yourself as a sexual being.

Sexual feelings are often intense. It is normal for an adolescent in puberty to have many questions, fears, and concerns about developing into a sexually mature adult. The eating illness often prevents the transition to sexual adulthood.

Your eating disorder interferes with healthy sexual growth for many reasons. Due to your compulsive overeating and obesity, you may feel ashamed of your body size and fearful that "no one would want me." Or you may be a compulsive noneater and still feel ashamed of your body size. Perhaps your fear of growing sexually mature is great. You may be uncomfortable with coming to know yourself as a sexual person. Maybe you have begun to realize that your sexual orientation is not heterosexual. Or you may have overwhelming desires to become sexually involved with many partners.

All women and men who are trying to achieve adulthood must face many of these issues. For the compulsive eater, however, the issues are often sidestepped or never addressed at all. That happens because the compulsive eater has learned to use eating or starving behavior to escape from other issues and to avoid facing life problems. The first time the compulsive eater begins to experience sexual feelings commonly happens shortly after the person becomes abstinent from compulsive eating/starving.

Some of you may have secrets about your sexual life that you don't want to tell others. You may have consciously or unconsciously used food to avoid dealing with your secrets. Perhaps you have experienced violent sexual behavior in the form of incest or rape. Maybe you have had sexual activity outside of marriage or with people of the same sex and find yourself feeling uncomfortable about it. Or, perhaps you have had many sexual partners or none at all and would like to change your behavior.

On my mind...
From the heart!

What issues do you need to talk about in regard to your sexual development and behavior? What are your worries or fears? Please write your thoughts here and then discuss them with your group:

_____

_____

_____

_____

_____

_____

_____

_____

_____

_____

_____

_____

_____

_____

_____

Some people are well organized in living their lives. They plan what to do in order to be effective in their work as well as in their personal lives. Sometimes they even make lists of "Things To Do Today" to help them stay on target.

Like the "organized" person, the recovering person needs to plan and do certain things to stay on target. Working at getting well and staying well is an ongoing task. Having a reprieve from your eating disorder means that you will plan and carry out the work of your recovery.

Look at the following list of "Things To Do Today." Give yourself a plus mark (+) next to the items you are now doing successfully. Put a check (✓) next to the items you need to work on today. At the bottom of the list, write your plan for action on three of the items that need work.

Things To Do Today

_____ Each morning, I ask God or my Higher Power to help me stay abstinent.

_____ I take a daily quiet time to pray and meditate.

_____ Every day I read literature from Overeaters, Narcotics, and/or Alcoholics Anonymous.

_____ I talk about my feelings with my peers.

_____ I follow my food plan.

_____ I am working the Twelve Steps of the OA program. Today I am working on Step _____.

_____ I practice living the slogans of the OA/AA programs.

_____ Each day I report my food plan to my OA sponsor.

_____ I have an OA home group.

_____ When I am preoccupied with symptoms of my eating disorder I telephone an OA member.

_____ When I am troubled, I ask for help.

_____ When I go to meetings, I talk about me and share my real feelings.

_____ I practice new ways to nurture myself. One thing that I do is _____

_____

_____ I am honest about my eating plan.

_____ I give service to others in OA.

_____ Today I practice living in the *present* moment.

_____ Occasionally, I make a gratitude list about my progress in recovery.

_____ I practice living in conscious contact with God or my Higher Power.

_____ I weigh myself only at planned intervals.

_____ Every evening I give thanks to my Higher Power for another day of abstinence.

PLAN FOR ACTION:

1. _____

_____

_____

2. _____

_____

_____

3. _____

_____

_____

What do you think about when you hear the word "recovery"? Take a minute and write your thoughts here: _____

_____

_____

_____

_____

To recover from an eating disorder is to receive a precious gift. It is getting a chance to begin again, to breathe freely, to laugh, to cry, to live! Recovery from your eating disorder will bring you a new serenity and peace that you have never known before. It will enable you to experience a profoundly animating joy. It will bring you to a rebirth of your spirit.

Are you still puzzled as to how this will happen to you? Reflect for a moment on the work you have done in this workbook. You have had to think and talk about the painful consequences of your eating illness. You have had to write and meditate and pray to begin to heal the wounds of your eating illness. You have had to ask for help, and you have had to hope and believe that recovery is happening to *you*.

Where are you now? What progress have you made toward taking a firm hold on your new life? On your recovery ?

Write your thoughts here and then share them with a friend:

_____

_____

_____

_____

_____

_____

Remember to live recovery today!

THE TWELVE STEPS

1. We admitted we were powerless over alcohol—that our lives had become unmanageable.

2. Came to believe that a Power greater than ourselves could restore us to sanity.

3. Made a decision to turn our will and our lives over to the care of God *as we understood Him.*

4. Made a searching and fearless moral inventory of ourselves.

5. Admitted to God, to ourselves, and to another human being the exact nature of our wrongs.

6. Were entirely ready to have God remove all these defects of character.

7. Humbly asked Him to remove our shortcomings.

8. Made a list of all persons we had harmed, and became willing to make amends to them all.

9. Made direct amends to such people wherever possible, except when to do so would injure them or others.

10. Continued to take personal inventory and when we were wrong promptly admitted it.

11. Sought through prayer and meditation to improve our conscious contact with God *as we understood Him,* praying only for knowledge of His will for us and the power to carry that out.

12. Having had a spiritual awakening as the result of these steps, we tried to carry this message to alcoholics, and to practice these principles in all our affairs.

© *The Twelve Steps.* Reprinted with permission of Alcoholics Anonymous World Services, Inc.

These steps have been adapted for use by many others, including Overeaters Anonymous.

More titles of interest . . .

Abstinence in Action
Food Planning for Compulsive Overeaters
by Barbara McFarland, Ed.D. and Anne Marie Erb
An essential tool for constructing a recovery plan, *Abstinence in Action* provides worksheets, activity records, and inventory checklists to help those in early recovery plan their meals and structure their time. An invaluable resource for assessing food use and tracking progress. 140 pp.
Order No. 5045

Food for Thought
Daily Meditations for Overeaters
by Elisabeth L.
Food for Thought offers guidance and inspiration to compulsive eaters. The meditations help those facing the challenges of early recovery to see the rewards of abstinence, rely on the wisdom of the Twelve Step program, and turn to their Higher Power for strength. 400 pp.
Order No. 1074

**For price and order information, or a free catalog,
please call our Telephone Representatives.**

1-800-328-0098	**1-651-213-4000**	**1-651-257-1331**
(Toll Free, U.S., Canada, and the Virgin Islands)	(Outside the U.S. and Canada)	(FAX) http://www.hazelden.org

Pleasant Valley Road • P.O. Box 176 • Center City, MN 55012-0176